# BOWIE HITS

FABER 𝆑𝆑 MUSIC

# ABSOLUTE BEGINNERS

Words and Music by David Bowie

bam,— bam, ba- ooh,            bam,— bam, ba-

-ooh.)

{ 1. I've no-thing much to of - fer,
  2. No-thing much could hap-pen,

there's no-thing much to take,
no-thing we can't shake,

I'm an ab - so - lute be - gin - ner,
oh, we're ab - so - lute be - gin - ners,

but we're ab - so - lute be - gin - ners,

{ with eyes com - plete - ly o - pen,
{ but if my love is your love,

but ner-vous all the same.
we're cer - tain to suc - ceed.

If our
If our

love song could fly o - ver moun - tains, could laugh at the
love song could fly o - ver moun - tains, could sail o - ver

# ALL THE YOUNG DUDES

Words and Music by David Bowie

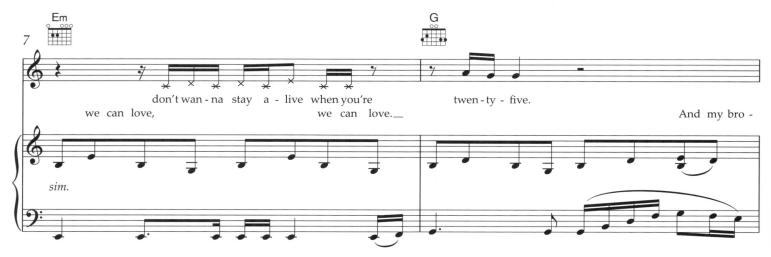

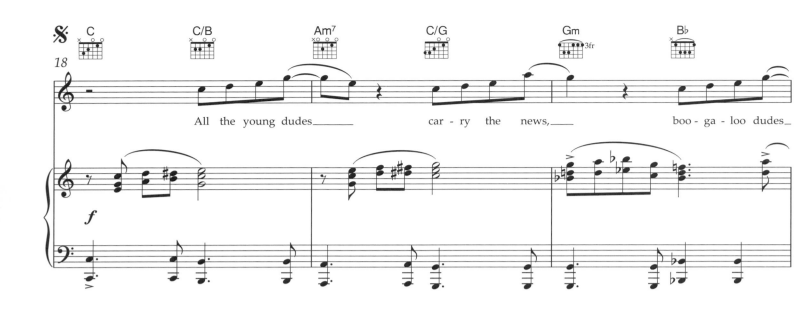

All the young dudes_____ car - ry the news,_____ boo - ga - loo dudes_

_____ car - ry the news._____ All the young dudes_

*(2° repeat back to 𝄋 and repeat chorus to fade)*

_____ car - ry the news,_____ boo - ga - loo dudes_____ car - ry the news._____ 2. Now

# AS THE WORLD FALLS DOWN

Words and Music by David Bowie

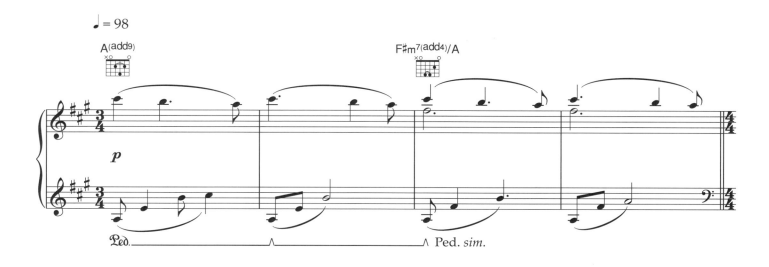

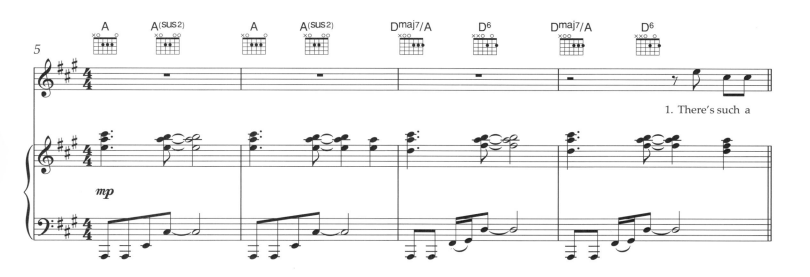

1. There's such a

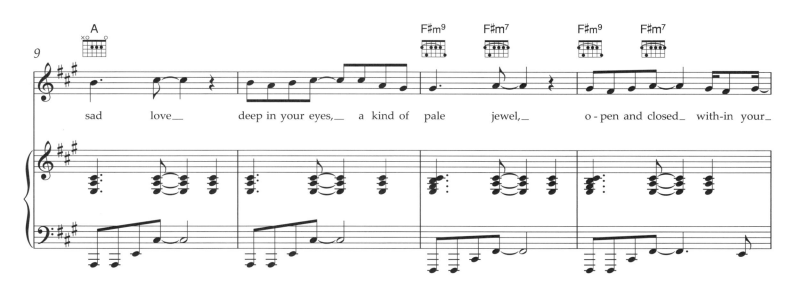

sad love___ deep in your eyes,___ a kind of pale jewel,___ o-pen and closed___ with-in your___

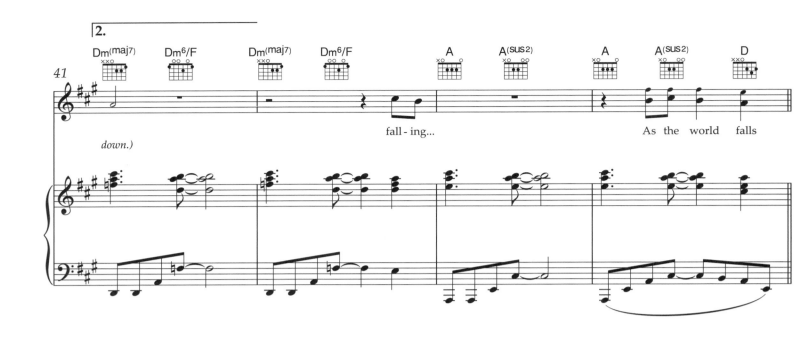

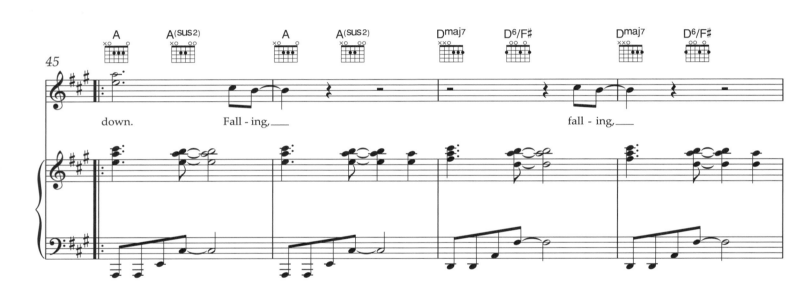

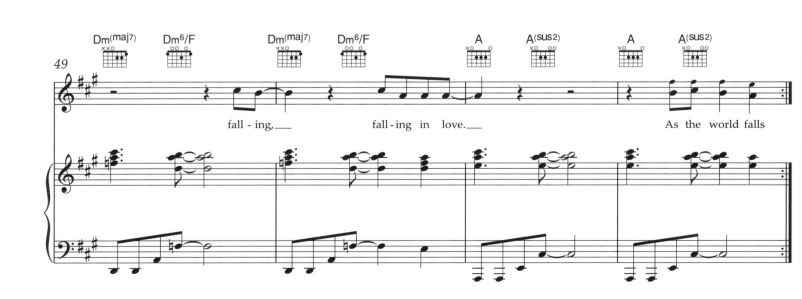

# ASHES TO ASHES

Words and Music by David Bowie

I've heard a ru - mour from Ground Con - trol, oh no, don't say it's true.__
but the lit - tle green wheels__ are fol - low - ing me,_____ oh no,___ not a - gain.__

They got a mes - sage from the Ac - tion Man, I'm hap - py, hope you're hap - py too,__
I'm stuck with a val - ua - ble friend:___ I'm hap - py, hope you're hap - py too,__

_____ I've loved all I've__ need - ed love,___ sor - did__ de - tails___ fol - low - ing:
_____ one flash of light but no smok - ing__ pis - tol.

The shriek - ing__ of no - thing is kill - ing, just pic - tures of Jap girls in syn - the - sis and I
I've ne - ver done good_____ things, I've ne - ver done bad_____ things,

My ma-ma said, to get things done, you'd bet-ter not mess with Ma - jor Tom.

(optional 8va)

(repeat ad lib. to fade)

# BLUE JEAN

*Words and Music by David Bowie*

1. Blue Jean    I just met a girl named Blue
2. One day    I'm gon-na write a po-em in a

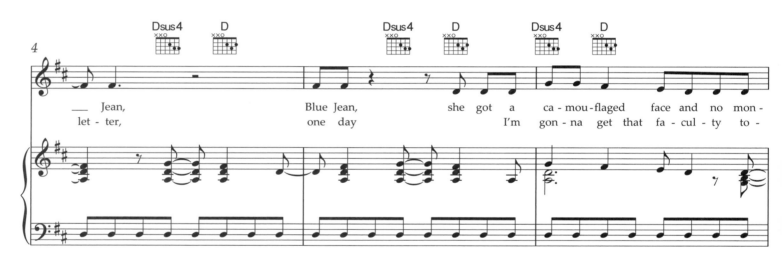

— Jean,    Blue Jean,    she got a ca-mou-flaged face and no mon-
let-ter,    one day    I'm gon-na get that fa-cul-ty to-

-ey.    Re-mem-ber,    they al-ways let you down__ when you
-geth-er.    Re-mem-ber,    that ev-'ry-bo-dy has to wait in

# BLACKSTAR

Words and Music by David Bowie

eyes.

Ah   ah   ah.

*mf*

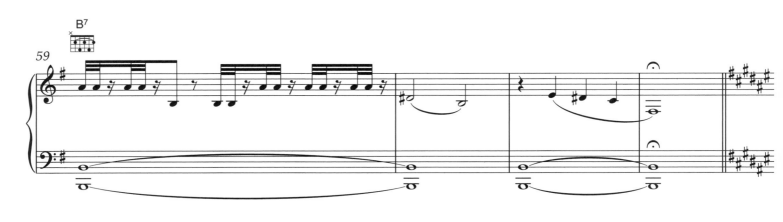

(ad lib.)

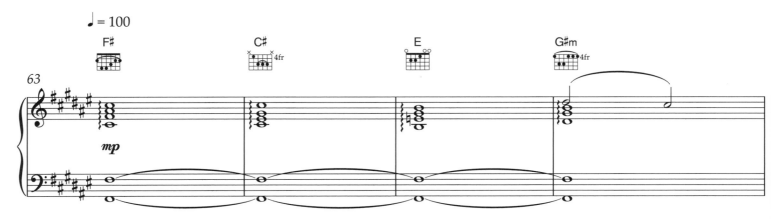

♩ = 100

*mp*

take you_ home,___ (I'm a black - star,)   take   your   pass-port_ and shoes,(I'm not a
born  up - side down,  (I'm a  star - star,)   born   the   wrong way_ round,___ (I'm not a

**1.**

pop - star,)   and___ your  sed - a - tives  boo,  (I'm  a  black - star,)   you're the

flash  in the pan,___ (I'm not a  Mar-vel - star,)__  I'm  the great I   Am,___  (I'm  a  black- star.)

# BEAUTY AND THE BEAST

Words and Music by David Bowie

Weav-ing down a by-road, sing-ing a song,— that's my kind of high-road

gone wrong.

My, my,— smile at least,— you can't say no__ to the

Beau-ty and the Beast.

Some-thing in the night, some-thing in the day, noth-ing is wrong__ but dar-ling

some-thing's in the way, there's slaugh-ter in the air, pro-test on the wind,

some-one else in-side me,___ some-one could get skinned, how?

(My,　　my,)__　　　some-one fetch a priest,　you can't　say　no__ to the

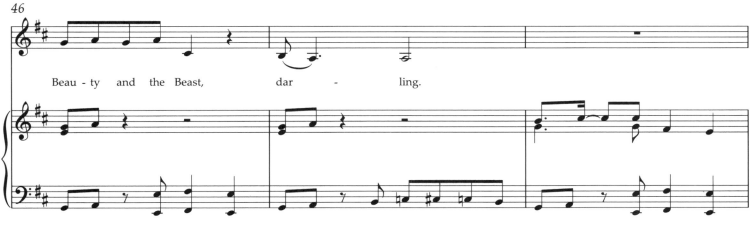

Beau - ty　and　the Beast,　　dar　-　ling.

*mf*

My, my,— you can't say no— to the Beau-ty and the Beast,

(lieb - ling.)

My, my,— you can't say no— to the Beau-ty and the Beast.

I want-ed to— be-lieve— me, I want-ed to be good,

I want-ed no___ dis - trac - tions, like ev -'ry good boy___ should.__

(My, my.)__

Noth - ing will cor - rupt us, noth - ing will com - pete, thank God hea - ven left us

stand - ing on our feet. My, my,___ Beau - ty and the

# BOYS KEEP SWINGING

Words and Music by David Bowie and Brian Eno

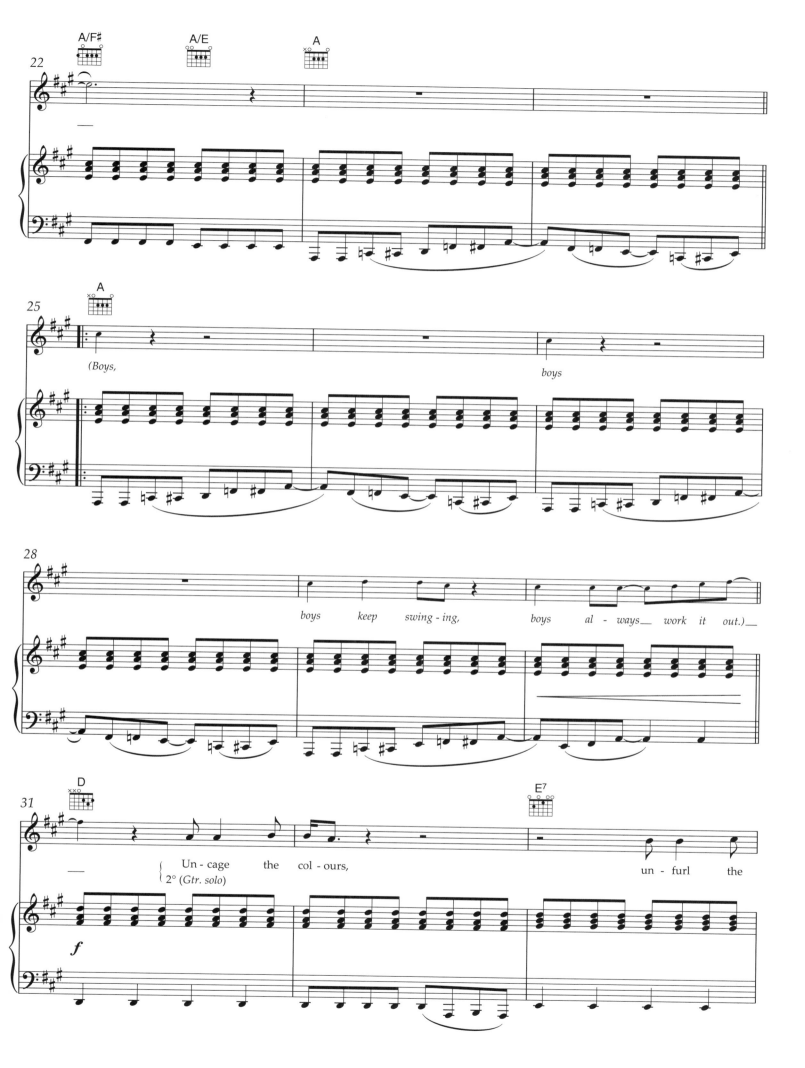

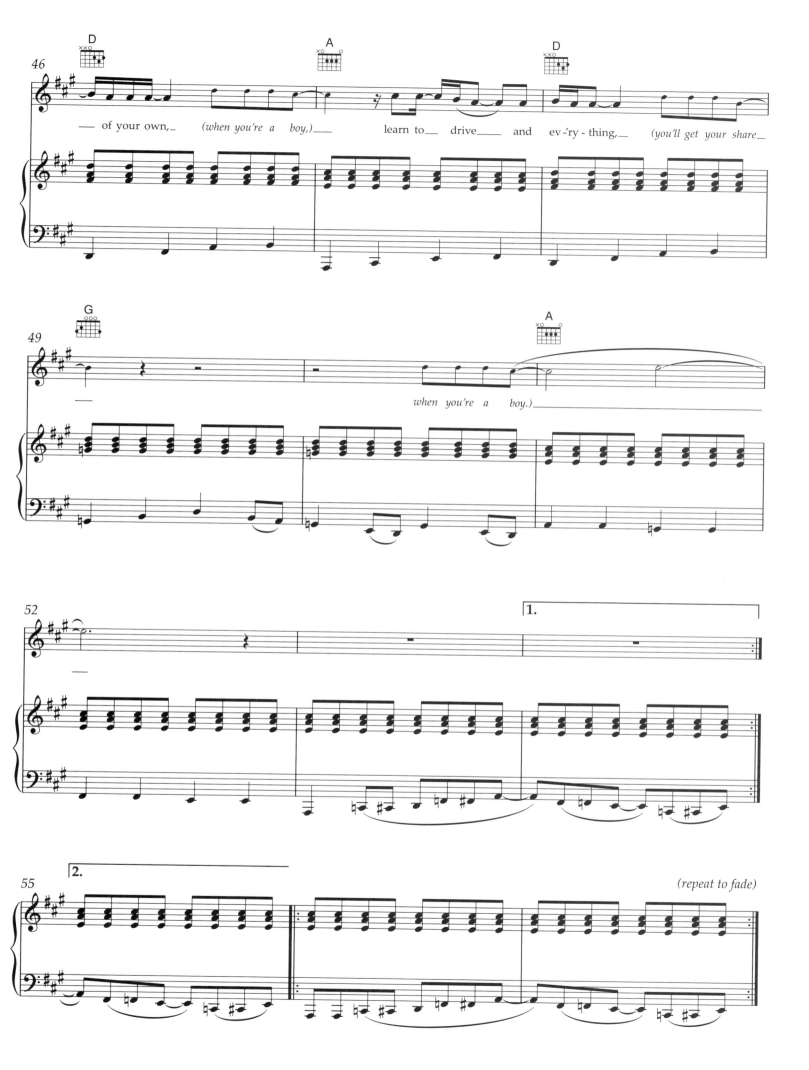

# CHANGES

Words and Music by David Bowie

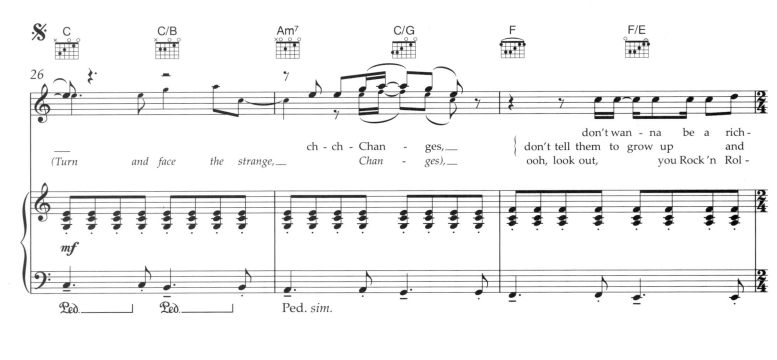

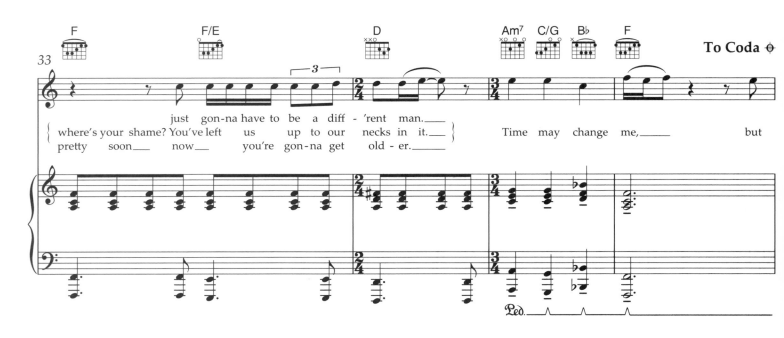

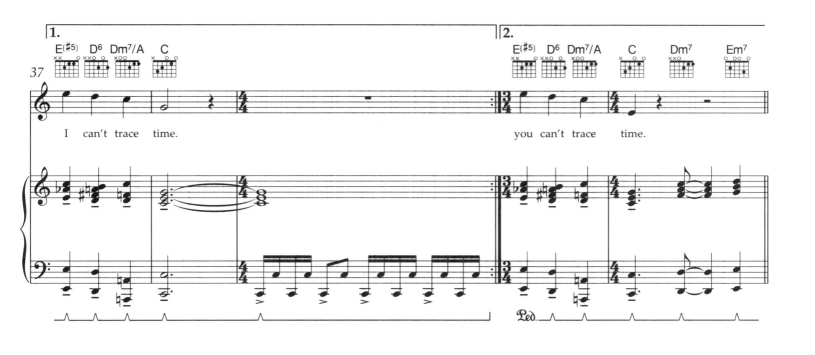

I can't trace time, I said that time may change me,_____ but I can't trace

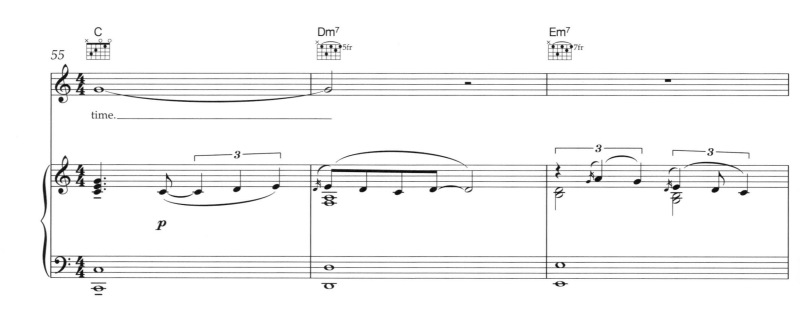

time._____

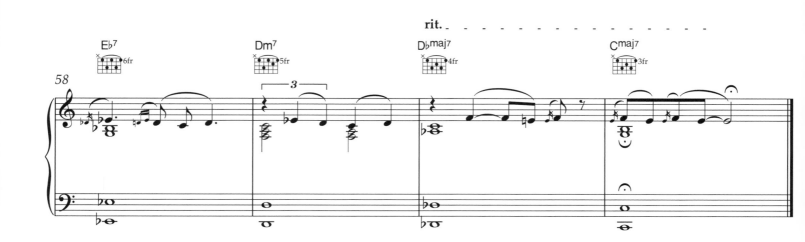

rit.

# CHINA GIRL

Words and Music by David Bowie and Iggy Pop

when I___ look at___ my Chi - na Girl.___

And I could pre - tend___ noth - ing real - ly___ meant___ too much,

when I___ look at___ my Chi - na Girl.___

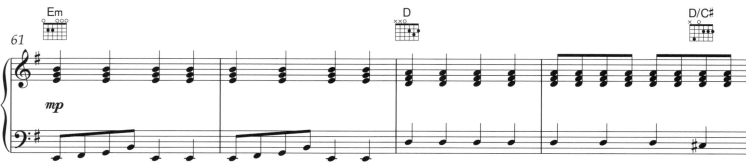

# DRIVE-IN SATURDAY

Words and Music by David Bowie

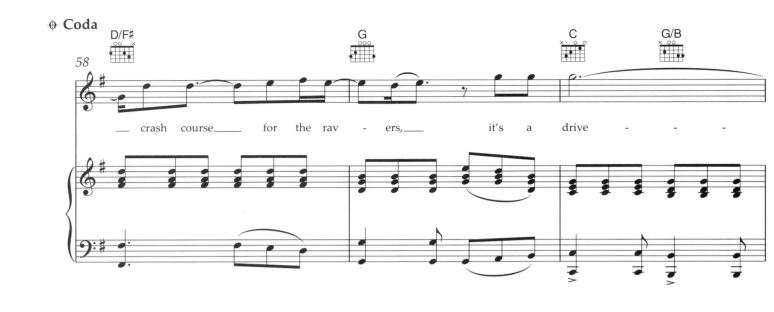

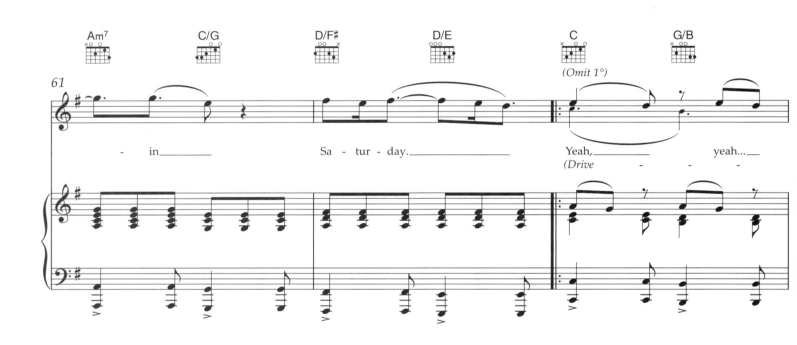

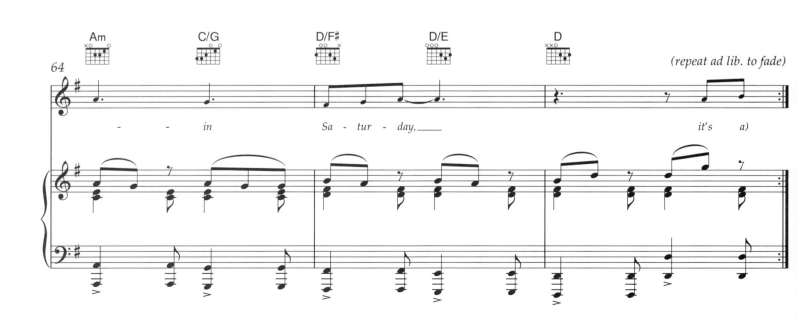

70

# EVERYONE SAYS 'HI'

Words and Music by David Bowie

# FASHION

Words and Music by David Bowie

(1.) brand new dance but I don't know its name,__ that
(2.) brand new talk but it's not ve-ry clear,__ (ooh bop,) that

# FIVE YEARS

Words and Music by David Bowie

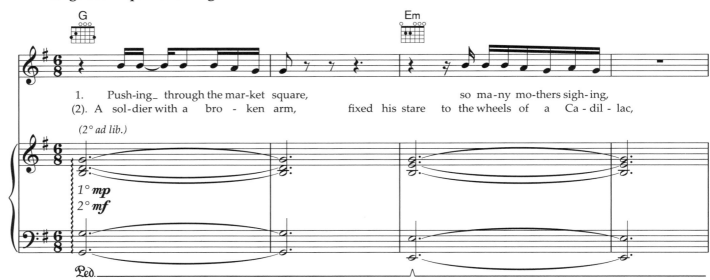

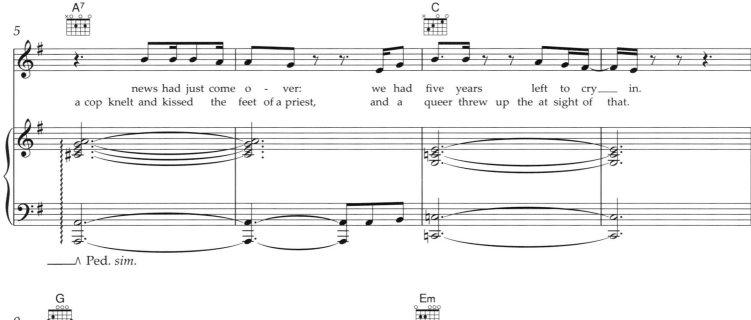

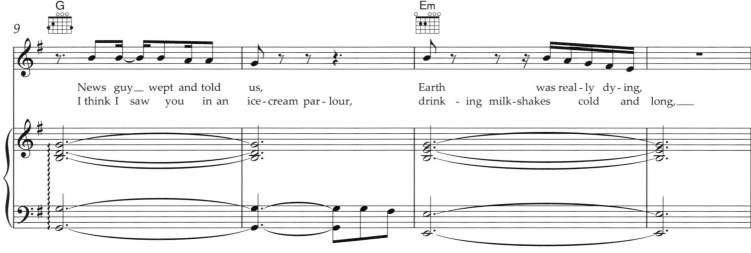

# FAME

Words and Music by John Lennon, David Bowie and Carlos Alomar

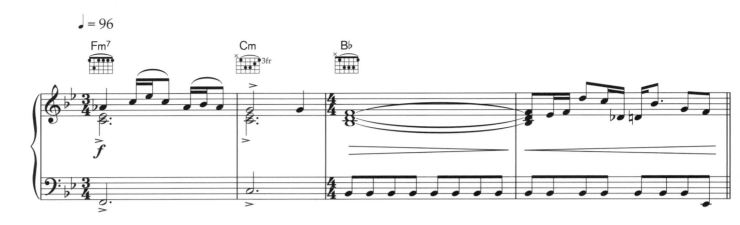

1. Fame,_____ makes a man__ take things o-ver, Fame,_____ lets him
2. Fame,_____ what you like__ is in the li-mo, Fame,_____ what you
3. Is it a-ny won-der__ I re-ject you first?_ Fame,_____ fame,__

loose, hard to swal-low, Fame,_____ puts you there__ where things are hol-low,
get is no to-mor-row, Fame,_____ what you need__ you have to bor-row,
fame,_____ fame,_ is it a-ny won-der__ you're__ too cool to fool?_

Fame._____
Fame._____ (Fame.)____
Fame._____ It's not yer brain, it's
"Nein, it's mine!" is
Bul-ly for you,_

just the flame__ that burns your change to keep you in - - sane._____
just his line__ to bind your time, it drives you to a crime._____
chilly for me,__ got - ta get a rain-check on pain._____

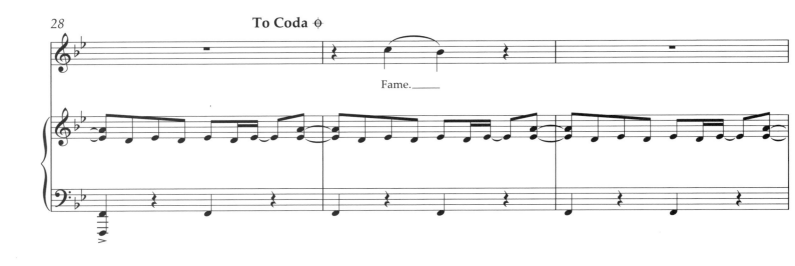

Fame.____

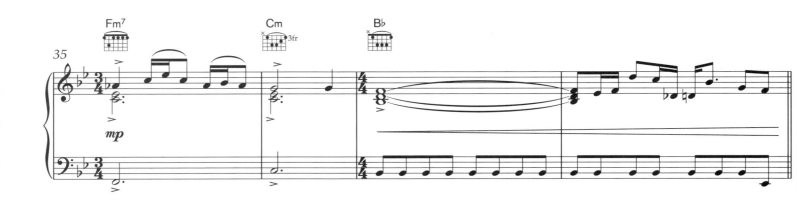

**D.𝄋 al Coda**

Do be da be da de,    do be da be,

do be da be,    do be da de,

do be da be da da,    do be da day,_____

_____    do be da de,    do be da de.

# "HEROES"

(Single Version)

Words by David Bowie
Music by David Bowie and Brian Eno

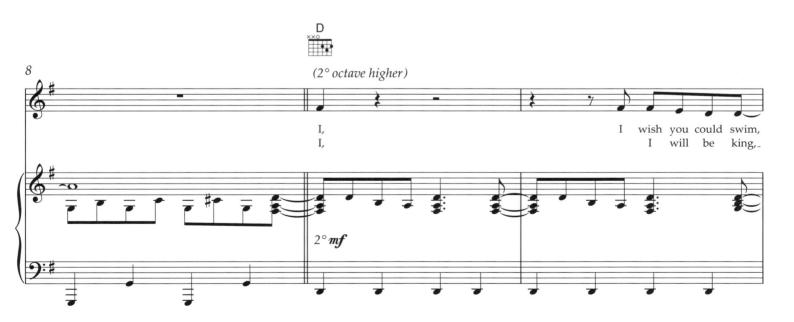

# GOLDEN YEARS

Words and Music by David Bowie

96

run for the sha - dows,____ run for the sha - dows in these gold - en years.)_

## Coda

gold - en years,____
(Gold - en years,_ gold,_____ whop whop whop,

gold - en

*(repeat ad lib. to fade)*

years,
gold - en years,_ gold,_____ whop whop whop.)

gold - en years.

# I CAN'T GIVE EVERYTHING AWAY

Words and Music by David Bowie

1, 4. I know something's very wrong, the pulse returns the prodigal sons,
2. Seeing more and feeling less, saying no but meaning yes,
3, 5. (Instrumental)

give    ev-'ry-thing                    a-

- way.

(repeat x4)

# THE JEAN GENIE

Words and Music by David Bowie

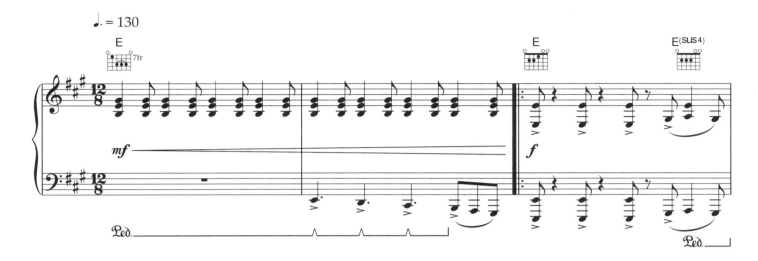

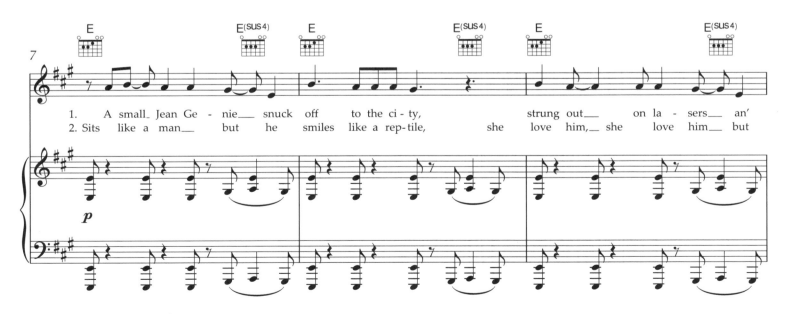

1. A small Jean Ge - nie__ snuck off to the ci - ty, strung out__ on la - sers__ an'
2. Sits like a man__ but he smiles like a rep-tile, she love him,__ she love him__ but

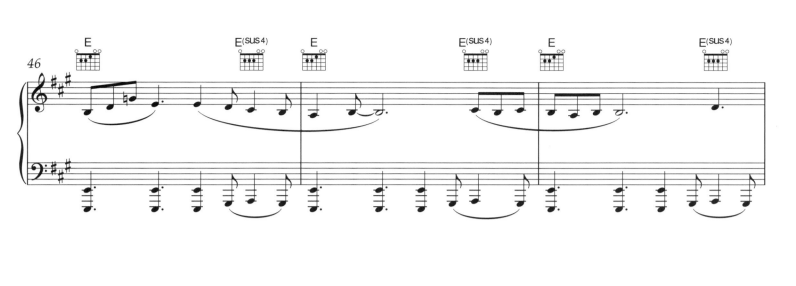

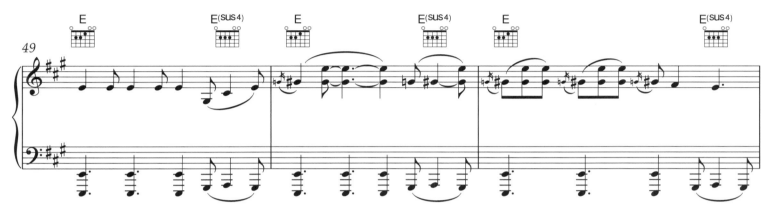

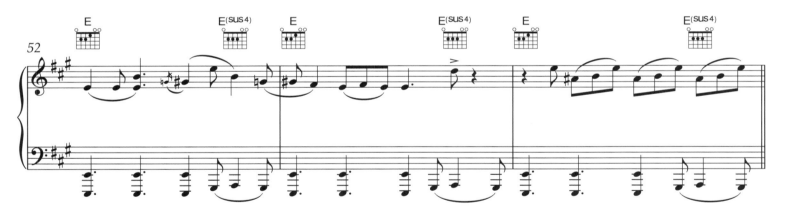

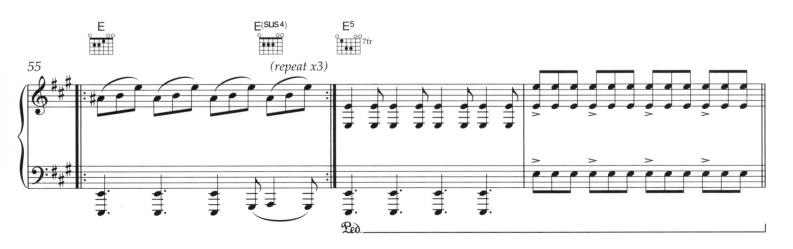

# JOHN, I'M ONLY DANCING

Words and Music by David Bowie

# LAZARUS

Words and Music by David Bowie

# LET'S DANCE

(Single Version)

Words and Music by David Bowie

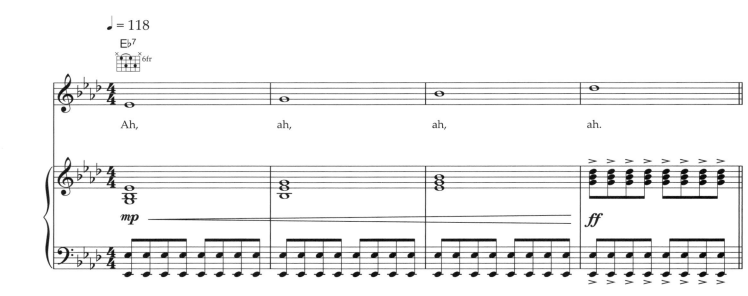

Ah,         ah,        ah,        ah.

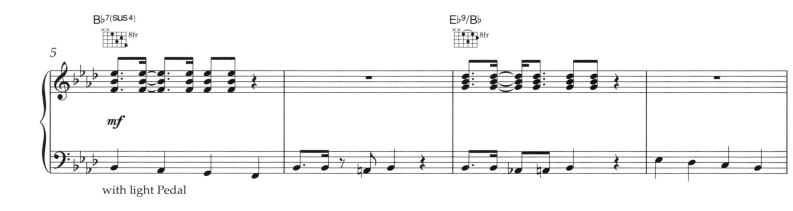

with light Pedal

1. (Let's

121

# LIFE ON MARS?

Words and Music by David Bowie

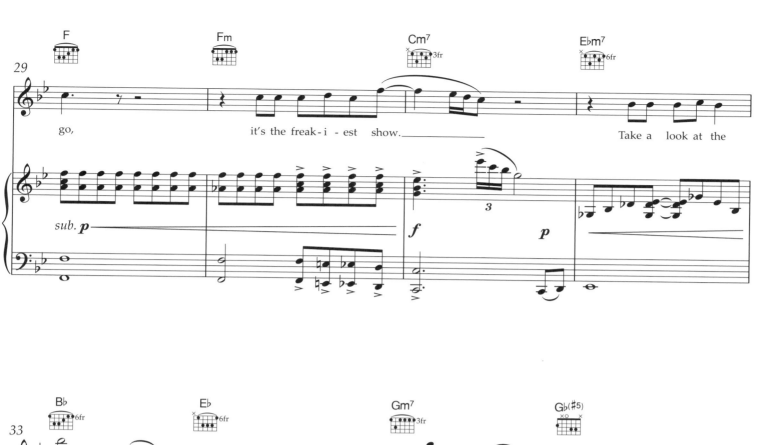

go,      it's the freak - i - est show._____      Take a   look at the

law - man\_\_   beat-ing up the wrong guy,\_\_   oh   man,\_\_   won-der if he'll e - ver know,

he's in the best sell - ing show._____      Is there life\_\_ on

Mars?

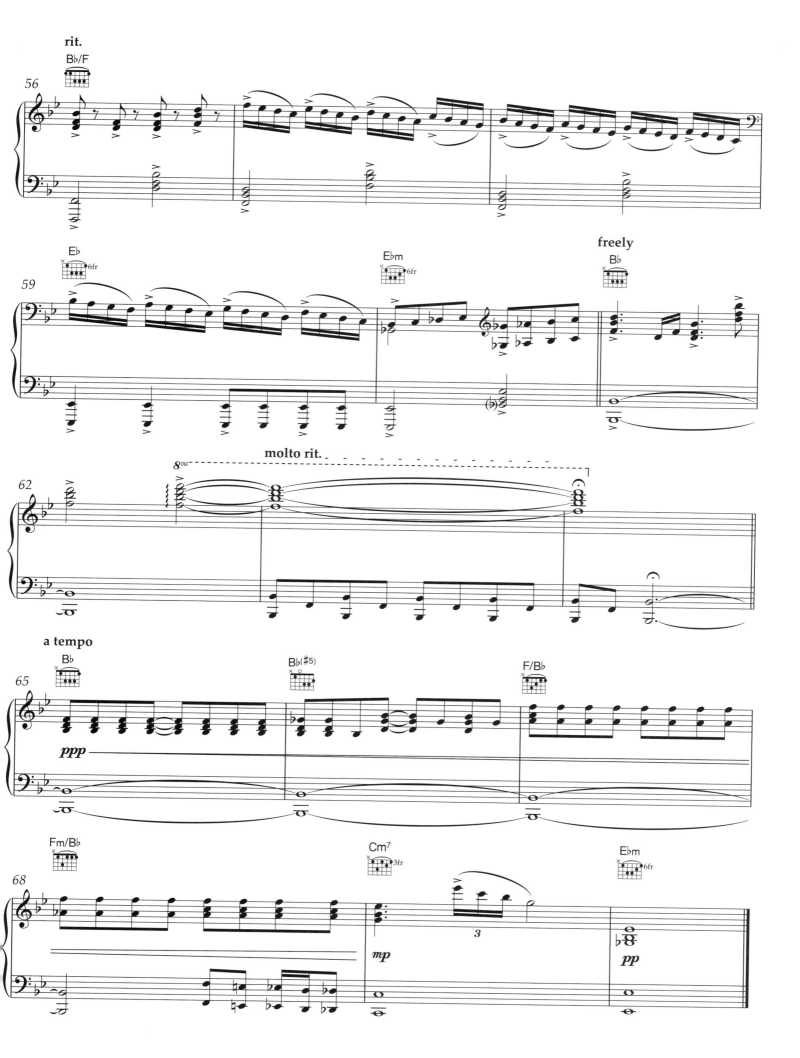

# LOVING THE ALIEN

(Single Version)

Words and Music by David Bowie

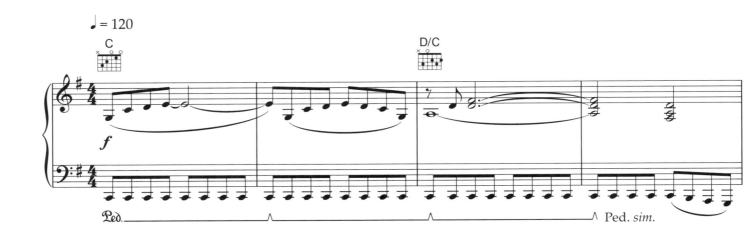

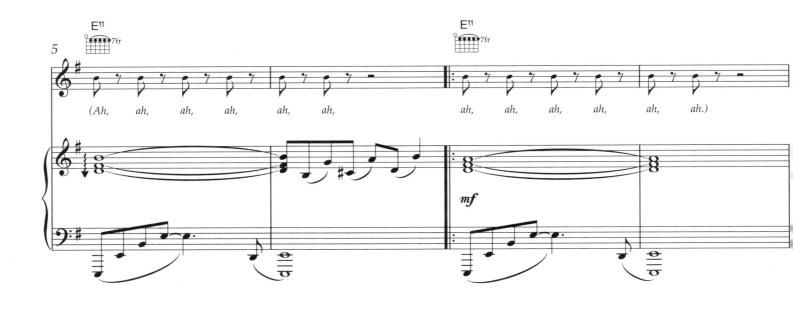

(Ah, ah, ah, ah, ah, ah, ah, ah, ah, ah, ah, ah.)

Be-liev-ing the strang - est things,____ lov-ing the a - li - en.____

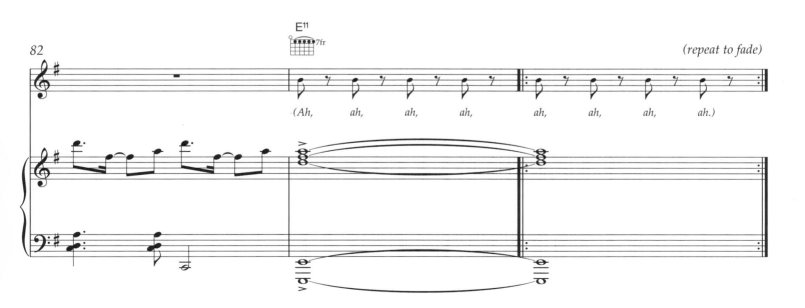

*(repeat to fade)*

(Ah, ah, ah, ah, ah, ah, ah, ah.)

135

# THE MAN WHO SOLD THE WORLD

Words and Music by David Bowie

# MODERN LOVE

Words and Music by David Bowie

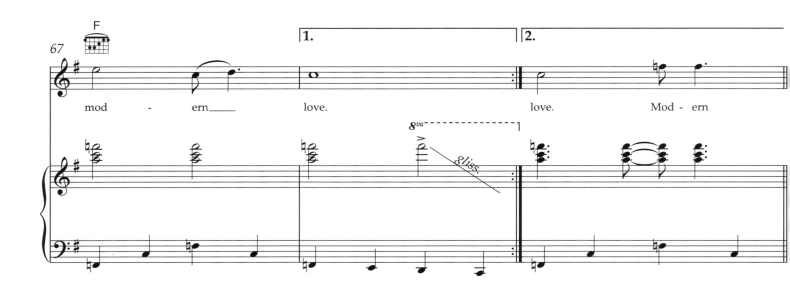

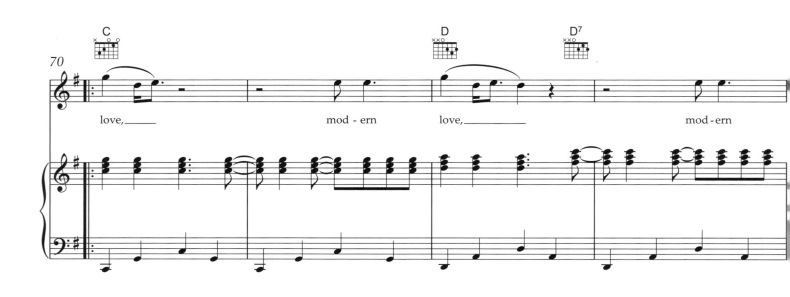

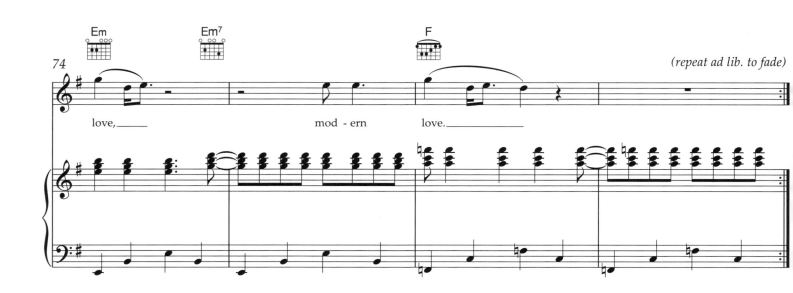

# MOONAGE DAYDREAM

Words and Music by David Bowie

make me, ba - by,____

make me know you real - ly care,_____ make me jump in - to the air._____

Keep your e - lec - tric eye____ on me, babe,__

put your ray-gun to my_____ head,_____

press your space face close__ to mine,___ love,__

freak out in a moon-age day-dream, oh_____ yeah._____

# NEW KILLER STAR

Words and Music by David Bowie

1. See the great white scar,        o - ver Bat - te - ry Park,___
2. See my life in a com - ic,      like the way they did the Bi - ble,

154

# OH! YOU PRETTY THINGS

Words and Music by David Bowie

1. Wake up you sleep-y head,

put on some clothes, shake up___ your bed, put an-oth-er log on the fire_____ for me,___

got-ta make way for the Ho-mo Su - pe - ri - or._____ 3. Look out at your chil-dren,

# REBEL REBEL

Words and Music by David Bowie

you're like me, and I like it all,___ we like danc-ing and we look div - ine,___

you love bands when they play it hard,___ you want more and you want it fast.___

They put you down, they say I'm wrong,_ you tack-y thing, you put them on.___

# SLOW BURN

Words and Music by David Bowie

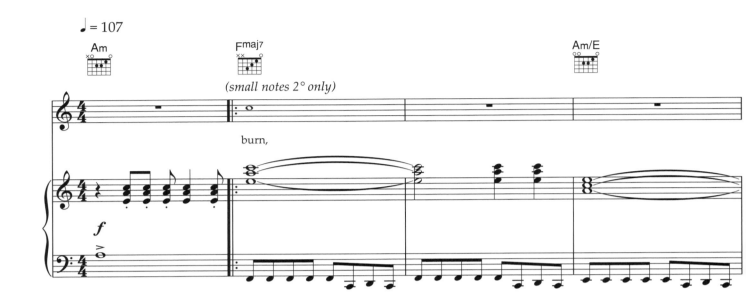

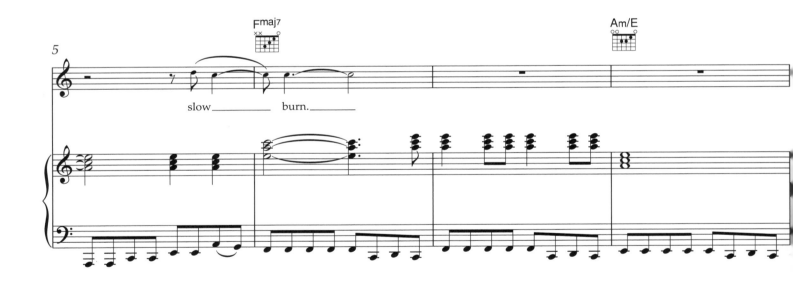

but we'll dance_____ in the dark,___ and they'll play_____ with our_ lives.__

who knows? Though the years____ snare____ them all.

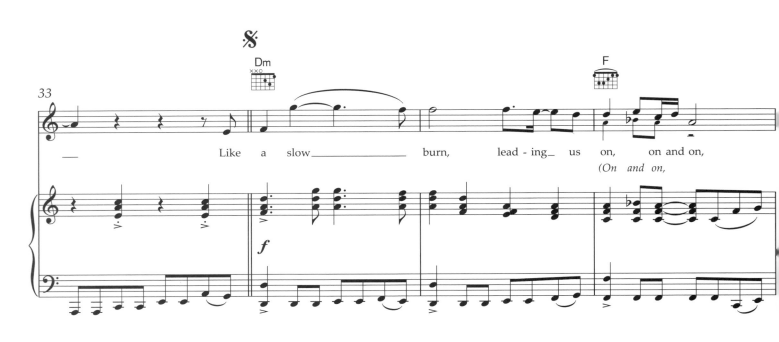

Like a slow_____ burn, lead-ing_ us on, on and on,

(On and on,

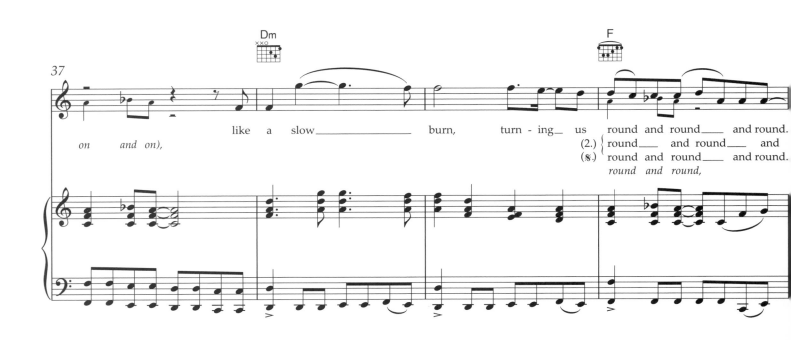

on and on), like a slow_____ burn, turn-ing_ us round and round____ and round.

(2.) round____ and round____ and

(%.) round and round____ and round.

round and round,

# SOUND AND VISION

Words and Music by David Bowie

# SPACE ODDITY

Words and Music by David Bowie

and the pa - pers want to know_ whose shirts you wear,_

now it's time to leave the cap - sule if you dare._

This is Ma - jor Tom_ to Ground Con - trol,_

I'm step - ping through the door,_____ and I'm

# STRANGERS WHEN WE MEET

Words and Music by David Bowie

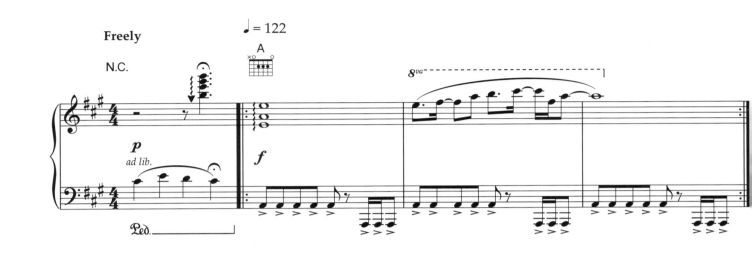

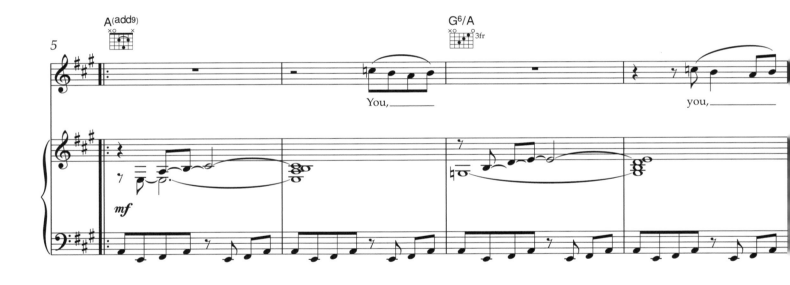

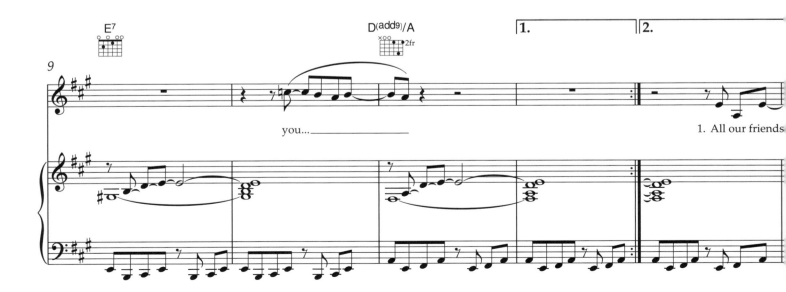

-ful,    for we're_    stran - gers when    we meet.

Cold,  tired

# SUFFRAGETTE CITY

Words and Music by David Bowie

189

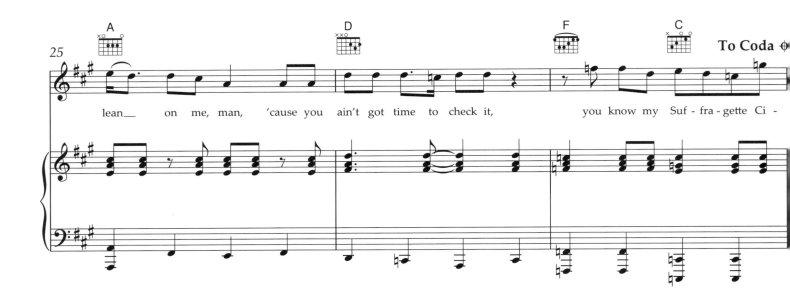

lean___ on me, man, 'cause you ain't got time to check it, you know my Suf - fra - gette Ci -

-ty___ is out - ta sight, she's al -

-right. Mmm.___

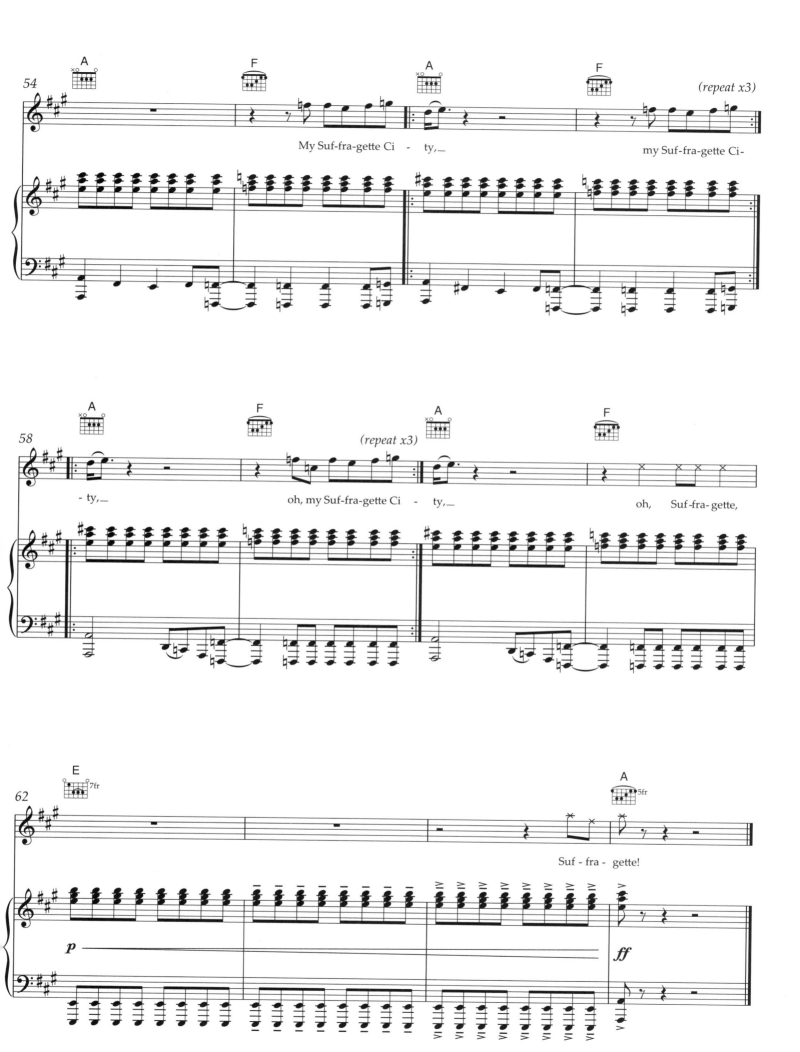

# STARMAN

Words and Music by David Bowie

told us not to blow it 'cause he knows___ it's all worth-while, he told___ me:___ "Let the chil-dren lose it, let the chil-dren use it, let all the chil-dren boo-gie."

La la___ la la la, la___ la la la, la___ la la la, la___ la la.

*(repeat ad lib. to fade)*

# THIS IS NOT AMERICA

from the Major Motion Picture Film *Falcon and the Snowman*

Words and Music by David Bowie, Pat Metheny and Lyle Mays

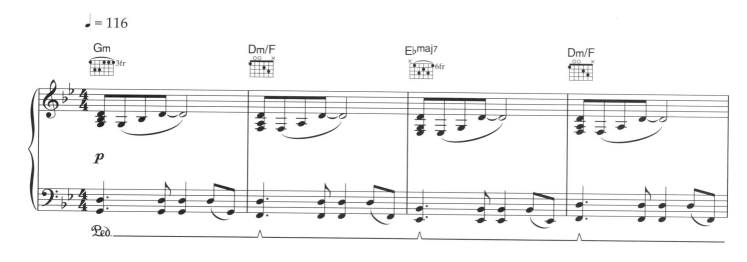

(This is not A - me - ri - ca, sha, la, la, la,

la.) A lit-tle piece_ of you, the lit-tle peace_ in me will_

die, _____ for_____ this is not A - me - ri - ca. _____
*(This is not a mi - ra - cle.)*

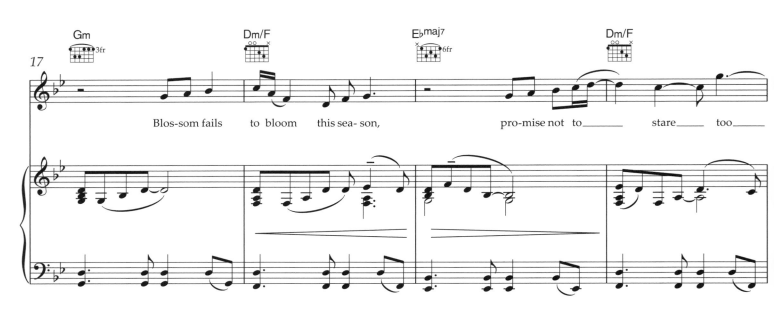

Blos-som fails to bloom this sea- son, pro-mise not to_____ stare_____ too_____

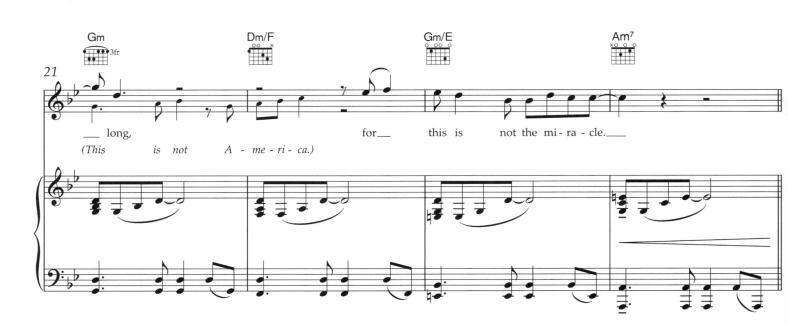

_____ long, for_____ this is not the mi - ra - cle. _____
*(This is not A - me - ri - ca.)*

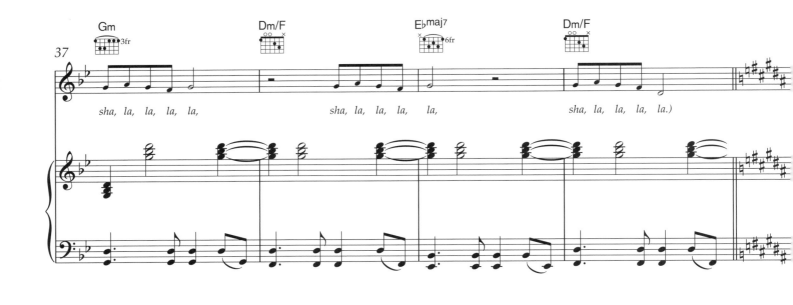

sha, la, la, la, la,     sha, la, la, la, la,     sha, la, la, la, la.)

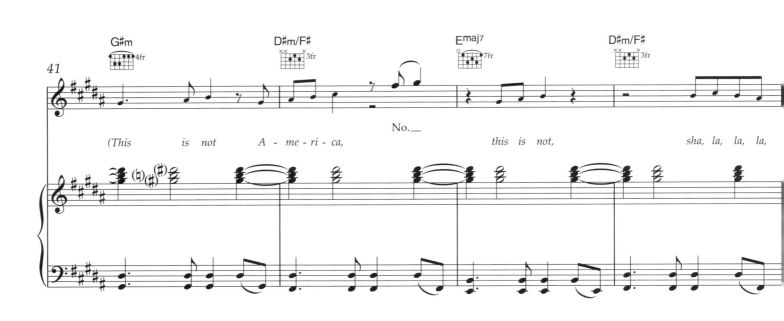

No.__

(This is not A - me - ri - ca,     this is not,     sha, la, la, la,

Snow - man_melt - ing from __ the in - side,_     fal - con_ spi - rals___ to_____ the__

la.)

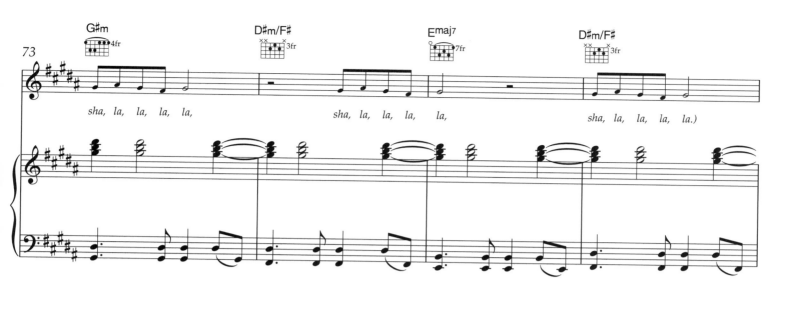

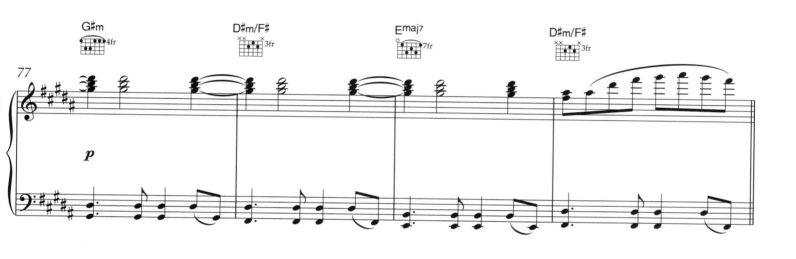

# THURSDAY'S CHILD

Words and Music by David Bowie and Reeves Gabrels

1. All of my life____ I've tried_ so hard,____ do-ing my best____ with what_ I had,____
2. Some-times I cried____ my heart_ to sleep,____ shuf-fl-ing days____ and lone - some nights,____

____ noth- ing much hap - pened all__ the same.____
____ some-times my cour - age fell_ to my feet.____

# UNDER PRESSURE

Words and Music by Freddie Mercury, Brian May, Roger Taylor, John Deacon and David Bowie

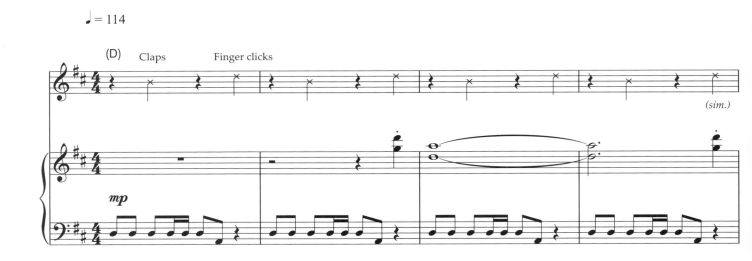

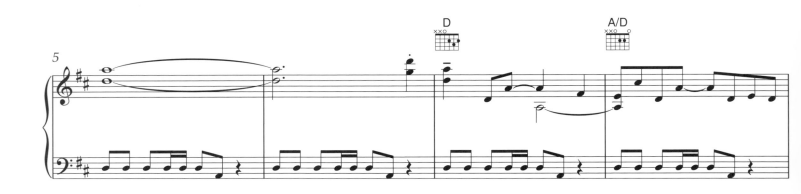

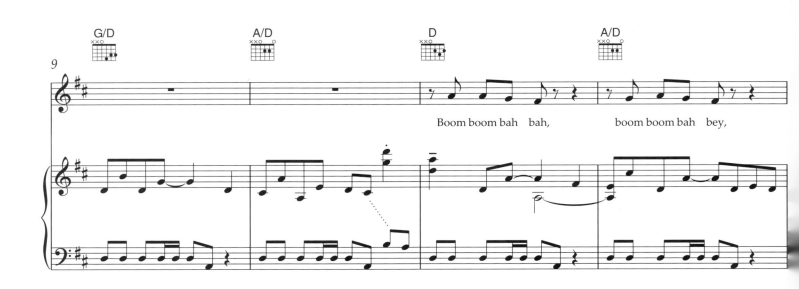

# YOUNG AMERICANS

(Single Version)

Words and Music by David Bowie

# WHERE ARE WE NOW?

Words and Music by David Bowie

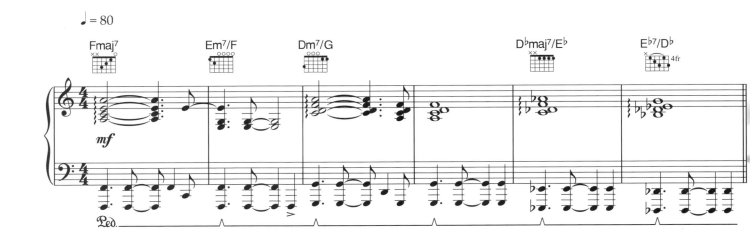

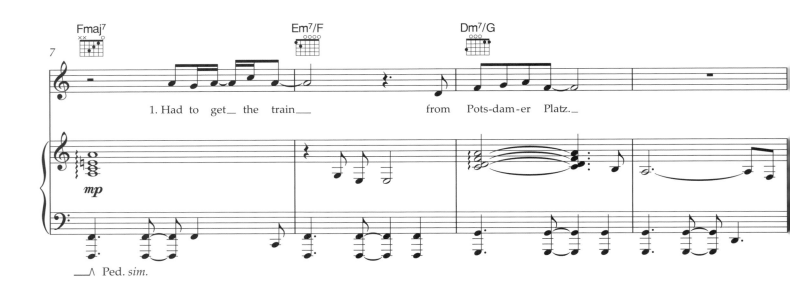

1. Had to get the train from Pots-dam-er Platz.

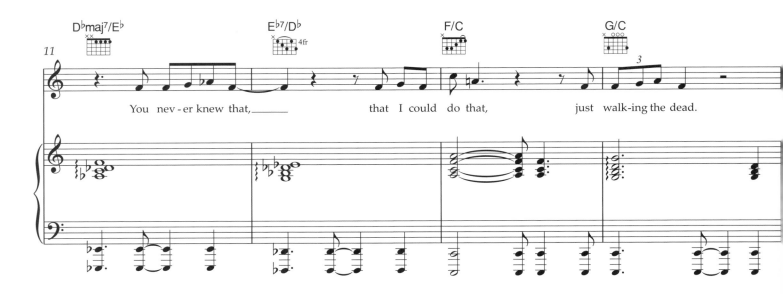

You nev-er knew that, that I could do that, just walk-ing the dead.

# ZIGGY STARDUST

Words and Music by David Bowie

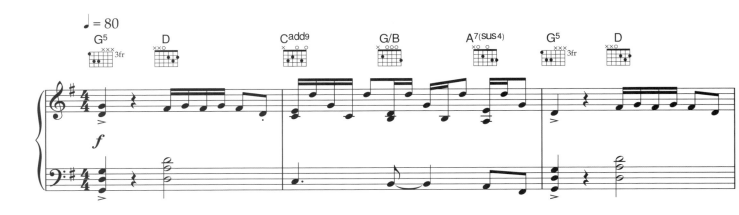

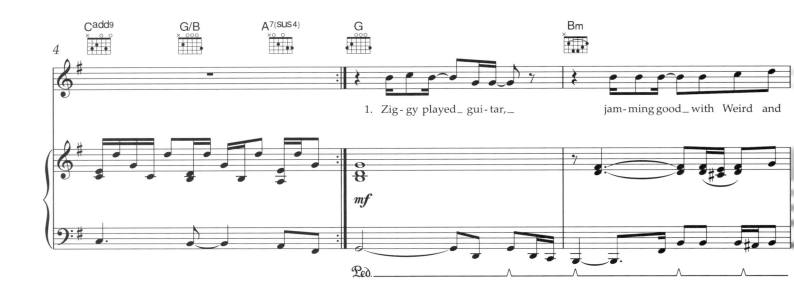

# TVC15

(Single Version)

Words and Music by David Bowie

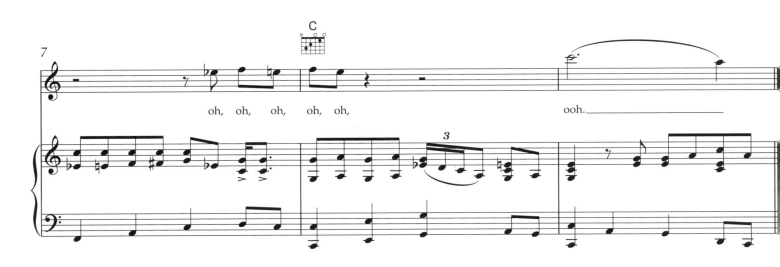

© 2023 by Faber Music Ltd.
First published in 2023 by Faber Music Ltd.
Brownlow Yard
12 Roger Street
London WC1N 2JU

Front cover photograph © Masayoshi Sukita, New York, 1973
Back cover contact sheet © Terry O'Neill / Iconic Images
Cover design by Adam Hay Studio
Music arranged by Olly Weeks
Compiled and edited by Lucy Holliday

Printed and bound in Turkey by Imago
All rights reserved.

ISBN 1: 0-571-54291-3
EAN 13: 978-0-571-54291-8

To buy Faber Music publications or to find out about the full range of titles available
please contact your local music retailer or Faber Music sales enquiries:

Faber Music Limited, Burnt Mill, Elizabeth Way, Harlow, CM20 2HX England
Tel: +44 (0)1279 82 89 82
fabermusic.com